MY IDEAS
Are as Bright as the Stars

Weekly Journal

Jennifer C. Petersen

MY IDEAS

Are as bright as the stars

This journal belongs to:

_____

"The best way to have a good idea is to have a lot of ideas." ~ Dr. Linus Pauling

You're smarter than you think you are!

You know how you wake up in the middle of the night with great ideas and have forgotten them by morning? Now you can keep track of those bright, sparkly ideas in a journal.

Did you participate in a weekly mastermind group? What topics did you discuss, what ideas did you have, what stood out for you (sparkles), what goals did you plan and what new things will you try? Write them all down and keep yourself accountable.

You'll notice the weeks are not dated. Sometimes life interferes and we miss a week. If that happens to you, just pick up where you left off and meet those goals – spark some new ideas and more importantly, achieve your dreams.
The sky is the limit. ~
Jennifer C. Petersen

This book or any portion thereof may not be reproduced or used in any manner whatsoever without the express written permission of the publisher except for the use of brief quotations in a book review.

Disclaimer and Terms of Use:

The Author and Publisher has strived to be as accurate and complete as possible in the creation of this book, notwithstanding the fact that she does not warrant or represent at any time that the contents within are accurate due to the rapidly changing nature of the contents and the Internet. While all attempts have been made to verify information provided in this publication, the Author and Publisher assumes no responsibility for errors, omissions, or contrary interpretation of the subject matter herein. Any perceived slights of specific persons, people, or organization are unintentional.

Printed in the United States of America.

First Printing, 2019

Tea Trade Mart Publishing
800 NE Tenney Rd 110-429
Vancouver, WA 98685
www.TeaTradeMart.com

"The best way to have a good idea is to have a lot of ideas." ~ Dr. Linus Pauling

"You have within you the strength, the patience, and the passion for the stars to change the world." ~ Harriet Tubman

Date: ___/___/___

Out of my head and onto the page

Learning Focus

Reach these goals

Find it, try it

Sparkles

"The best way to have a good idea is to have a lot of ideas." ~ Dr. Linus Pauling

"Everyone is a genius at least once a year. The real geniuses simply have their bright ideas closer together." ~ George C. Lichtenberg

Date: ___/___/___

Out of my head and onto the page

Learning Focus

Reach these goals

Find it, try it

Sparkles

"I can't understand why people are frightened of new ideas. I'm frightened of the old ones." ~John Cage

Date: ___/___/___

Out of my head and onto the page

Learning Focus

Reach these goals

Find it, try it

Sparkles

"The best way to have a good idea is to have a lot of ideas." ~ Dr. Linus Pauling

"Leave a little sparkle wherever you go."

Date: ___/___/___

Out of my head and onto the page

Learning Focus

Reach these goals

Find it, try it

Sparkles

"The best way to have a good idea is to have a lot of ideas." ~ Dr. Linus Pauling

"Better a diamond with a flaw than a pebble without imperfections." ~ Confucius

Date: ___/___/___

Out of my head and onto the page

Learning Focus

Reach these goals

Find it, try it

Sparkles

"The best way to have a good idea is to have a lot of ideas." ~ Dr. Linus Pauling

"If at first the idea is not absurd, then there is no hope for it." ~ Albert Einstein

Date: ___/___/___

Out of my head and onto the page

Learning Focus

Reach these goals

Find it, try it

Sparkles

"The best way to have a good idea is to have a lot of ideas." ~ Dr. Linus Pauling

"A mediocre idea that generates enthusiasm will go further than a great idea that inspires no one." ~ Mary Kay Ash

Date: ___/___/___

Out of my head and onto the page

Learning Focus

Reach these goals

Find it, try it

Sparkles

"The best way to have a good idea is to have a lot of ideas." ~ Dr. Linus Pauling

"Creativity is not the finding of a thing, but the making something out of it after it is found." ~ James Russell Lowell

Date: ___/___/___

Out of my head and onto the page

Learning Focus

Reach these goals

Find it, try it

Sparkles

"The best way to have a good idea is to have a lot of ideas." ~ Dr. Linus Pauling

"No matter how good you think you are as a leader, the people around you will have

all kinds of ideas of how you can get better." ~Jim Yong Kim

Date: ___/___/___

Out of my head and onto the page

Learning Focus

Reach these goals

Find it, try it

Sparkles

"The best way to have a good idea is to have a lot of ideas." ~ Dr. Linus Pauling

"Great minds discuss ideas; average minds discuss events; small minds discuss people." ~ Eleanor Roosevelt

Date: ___/___/___

Out of my head and onto the page

Learning Focus

Reach these goals

Find it, try it

Sparkles

"The best way to have a good idea is to have a lot of ideas." ~ Dr. Linus Pauling

"The ability to convert ideas to things is the secret of outward success." ~ Henry Ward Beecher

Date: ___/___/___

Out of my head and onto the page

Learning Focus

Reach these goals

Find it, try it

Sparkles

"The best way to have a good idea is to have a lot of ideas." ~ Dr. Linus Pauling

"When all think alike, then no one is thinking." ~ Walter Lippman

Date: ___/___/___

Out of my head and onto the page

Learning Focus

Reach these goals

Find it, try it

Sparkles

"The best way to have a good idea is to have a lot of ideas." ~ Dr. Linus Pauling

"Ideas can be life changing. Sometimes all you need to open the door is just one more good idea." ~ Jim Rohn

Date: ___/___/___

Out of my head and onto the page

Learning Focus

Reach these goals

Find it, try it

Sparkles

"A pile of rocks ceases to be a rock when somebody contemplates it with the ideas of a cathedral in mind." ~ Antoine De St. Exupery

Date: ___/___/___

Out of my head and onto the page

Learning Focus

Reach these goals

Find it, try it

Sparkles

"The best way to have a good idea is to have a lot of ideas." ~ Dr. Linus Pauling

"There is only one thing that makes a dream impossible to achieve: the fear of failure." Paulo Coelho

Date: ___/___/___

Out of my head and onto the page

Learning Focus

Reach these goals

Find it, try it

Sparkles

"Do more of what makes your heart sing, your eyes sparkle, and your soul soar."

Date: ___/___/___

Out of my head and onto the page

Learning Focus

Reach these goals

Find it, try it

Sparkles

"The best way to have a good idea is to have a lot of ideas." ~ Dr. Linus Pauling

"Twenty years from now, you will be more disappointed by the things that you didn't do than by the ones you did do. So throw off the bowlines. Sail away from the Safe Harbor. Catch the trade winds in your sails. Explore. Dream. Discover." ~ Mark Twain

Date: ___/___/___

Out of my head and onto the page

Learning Focus

Reach these goals

Find it, try it

Sparkles

"The best way to have a good idea is to have a lot of ideas." ~ Dr. Linus Pauling

"The role of a creative leader is not to have all ideas; it's to create a culture where everyone can have ideas and feel that they're valued." ~ Ken Robinson

Date: ___/___/___

Out of my head and onto the page

Learning Focus

Reach these goals

Find it, try it

Sparkles

"The most fundamental thing about leadership is to have the humility to continue to get feedback and to try to get better - because your job is to help everybody else get better." ~ Jim Yong Kim

Date: ___/___/___

Out of my head and onto the page

Learning Focus

Reach these goals

Find it, try it

Sparkles

"The best way to have a good idea is to have a lot of ideas." ~ Dr. Linus Pauling

"A library is the delivery room for the birth of ideas, a place where history comes to life." ~ Norman Cousins

Date: ___/___/___

Out of my head and onto the page

Learning Focus

Reach these goals

Find it, try it

Sparkles

"The best way to have a good idea is to have a lot of ideas." ~ Dr. Linus Pauling

"It's not really about the competition. Your biggest challenge in a race is yourself." ~ Summer Sanders

Date: ___/___/___

Out of my head and onto the page

Learning Focus

Reach these goals

Find it, try it

Sparkles

"Be less curious about people and more curious about ideas." ~ Marie Curie

Date: ___/___/___

Out of my head and onto the page

Learning Focus

Reach these goals

Find it, try it

Sparkles

"The best way to have a good idea is to have a lot of ideas." ~ Dr. Linus Pauling

"Collaboration is like carbonation for fresh ideas. Working together bubbles up ideas you would not have come up with solo, which gets you further faster." ~ Caroline Ghosn

Date: ___/___/___

Out of my head and onto the page

Learning Focus

Reach these goals

Find it, try it

Sparkles

"Enthusiasm is the yeast that makes your hopes shine to the stars. Enthusiasm is the sparkle in your ideas, the swing in your gait.

The grip of your hand, the irresistible urge of will and energy to execute your ideas." ~ Henry Ford

Date: ___/___/___

Out of my head and onto the page

Learning Focus

Reach these goals

Find it, try it

Sparkles

"The best way to have a good idea is to have a lot of ideas." ~ Dr. Linus Pauling

"Creativity comes from a conflict of ideas." ~ Donatella Versace

Date: ___/___/___

Out of my head and onto the page

Learning Focus

Reach these goals

Find it, try it

Sparkles

"Ideas are like pizza dough, made to be tossed around." ~ Anna Quindlen

Date: ___/___/___

Out of my head and onto the page

Learning Focus

Reach these goals

Find it, try it

Sparkles

"I like to think of ideas as potential energy.

They're really wonderful, but nothing will happen until we risk putting them into action." ~ Mae Jemison

Date: ___/___/___

Out of my head and onto the page

Learning Focus

Reach these goals

Find it, try it

Sparkles

"The best way to have a good idea is to have a lot of ideas." ~ Dr. Linus Pauling

"Nothing can dim the light that shines from within." ~ Maya Angelou

Date: ___/___/___

Out of my head and onto the page

Learning Focus

Reach these goals

Find it, try it

Sparkles

"The best way to have a good idea is to have a lot of ideas." ~ Dr. Linus Pauling

"In the realm of ideas, everything depends on enthusiasm....in the real world all rests on perseverance." ~ Johann Wolfgang von Goethe

Date: ___/___/___

Out of my head and onto the page

Learning Focus

Reach these goals

Find it, try it

Sparkles

"The best way to have a good idea is to have a lot of ideas." ~ Dr. Linus Pauling

"Our heritage and ideals, our code and standards - the things we live by and teach our children —

are preserved or diminished by how freely we exchange ideas and feelings." ~ Walt Disney

Date: ___/___/___

Out of my head and onto the page

Learning Focus

Reach these goals

Find it, try it

Sparkles

"The best way to have a good idea is to have a lot of ideas." ~ Dr. Linus Pauling

"Even a fool knows you can't touch the stars, but it won't keep the wise from trying." ~ Harry Anderson

Date: ___/___/___

Out of my head and onto the page

Learning Focus

Reach these goals

Find it, try it

Sparkles

"The best way to have a good idea is to have a lot of ideas." ~ Dr. Linus Pauling

"We need to give each other space so that we may both give and receive such beautiful things as ideas, openness, dignity, joy, healing, and inclusion." ~ Max de Pree

Date: ___/___/___

Out of my head and onto the page

Learning Focus

Reach these goals

Find it, try it

Sparkles

"Every time you tear a leaf off a calendar, you present a new place for new ideas and progress." ~ Charles Kettering

Date: ___/___/___

Out of my head and onto the page

Learning Focus

Reach these goals

Find it, try it

Sparkles

"The best way to have a good idea is to have a lot of ideas." ~ Dr. Linus Pauling

"Ideas shape the course of history." ~ John Maynard Keynes

Date: ___/___/___

Out of my head and onto the page

Learning Focus

Reach these goals

Find it, try it

Sparkles

"The best way to have a good idea is to have a lot of ideas." ~ Dr. Linus Pauling

"I'm open for possibilities. I'm open for choices. I'm always eager to learn. I'm never going to close my mind from learning." ~ Cesar Milan

Date: ___/___/___

Out of my head and onto the page

Learning Focus

Reach these goals

Find it, try it

Sparkles

"Unleash your inner sparkle!"

Date: ___/___/___

Out of my head and onto the page

Learning Focus

Reach these goals

Find it, try it

Sparkles

"Keep your feet on the ground and keep reaching for the stars." ~ Casey Kasem

Date: ___/___/___

Out of my head and onto the page

Learning Focus

Reach these goals

Find it, try it

Sparkles

"The best way to have a good idea is to have a lot of ideas." ~ Dr. Linus Pauling

"Don't let anyone dim your light simply because it's shining in their eyes."

Date: ___/___/___

Out of my head and onto the page

Learning Focus

Reach these goals

Find it, try it

Sparkles

"A star doesn't ask if it can shine, it just does."

Date: ___/___/___

Out of my head and onto the page

Learning Focus

Reach these goals

Find it, try it

Sparkles

"We are all of us stars and we deserve to twinkle." ~ Marilyn Monroe

Date: ___/___/___

Out of my head and onto the page

Learning Focus

Reach these goals

Find it, try it

Sparkles

"The best way to have a good idea is to have a lot of ideas." ~ Dr. Linus Pauling

"Dream big. Sparkle more. Shine bright."

Date: ___/___/___

Out of my head and onto the page

Learning Focus

Reach these goals

Find it, try it

Sparkles

"Look up at the stars and not down at your feet. Try to make sense of what you see, and wonder about what makes the universe exist. Be curious." ~ Stephen Hawking

Date: ___/___/___

Out of my head and onto the page

Learning Focus

Reach these goals

Find it, try it

Sparkles

"The best way to have a good idea is to have a lot of ideas." ~ Dr. Linus Pauling

"I'm a dreamer. I have to dream and reach for the stars, and if I miss a star then I grab a handful of clouds." ~ Mike Tyson

Date: ___/___/___

Out of my head and onto the page

Learning Focus

Reach these goals

Find it, try it

Sparkles

"The best way to have a good idea is to have a lot of ideas." ~ Dr. Linus Pauling

"It is not in the stars to hold our destiny but in ourselves." ~ William Shakespeare

Date: ___/___/___

Out of my head and onto the page

Learning Focus

Reach these goals

Find it, try it

Sparkles

"Shoot for the moon and if you miss, you will still be among the stars." ~ Les Brown

Date: ___/___/___

Out of my head and onto the page

Learning Focus

Reach these goals

Find it, try it

Sparkles

"The best way to have a good idea is to have a lot of ideas." ~ Dr. Linus Pauling

"For my part, I know nothing with any certainty, but the sight of the stars makes me dream." ~ Vincent Van Gogh

Date: ___/___/___

Out of my head and onto the page

Learning Focus

Reach these goals

Find it, try it

Sparkles

"The best way to have a good idea is to have a lot of ideas." ~ Dr. Linus Pauling

"God writes the Gospel not in the Bible alone, but also in trees, and in the flowers and clouds and stars." ~ Martin Luther

Date: ___/___/___

Out of my head and onto the page

Learning Focus

Reach these goals

Find it, try it

Sparkles

"No pessimist ever discovered the secret of the stars,

or sailed to an uncharted land, or opened a new doorway for the human spirit," ~ Helen Keller

Date: ___/___/___

Out of my head and onto the page

Learning Focus

Reach these goals

Find it, try it

Sparkles

"The best way to have a good idea is to have a lot of ideas." ~ Dr. Linus Pauling

"Jump into the middle of things, get your hands dirty, fall flat on your face, and then reach for the stars." ~ Ben Stein

Date: ___/___/___

Out of my head and onto the page

Learning Focus

Reach these goals

Find it, try it

Sparkles

"Stretching his hand up to reach the stars, too often man forgets the flowers at his feet." ~ Jeremy Bentham

Date: ___/___/___

Out of my head and onto the page

Learning Focus

Reach these goals

Find it, try it

Sparkles

"The best way to have a good idea is to have a lot of ideas." ~ Dr. Linus Pauling

"Be glad of life because it gives you the change to love, to work, to play, and to look up at the stars." ~ Henry Van Dyke

Date: ___/___/___

Out of my head and onto the page

Learning Focus

Reach these goals

Find it, try it

Sparkles

"The best way to have a good idea is to have a lot of ideas." ~ Dr. Linus Pauling

RECOMMENDATIONS

Other Books by Jennifer C. Petersen

Available on Amazon

http://www.amazon.com/Jennifer-C.-Petersen

17-76 Tea Party Award Winning Recipes

      17 Jam and Scone Recipes

      Foreword by James Norwood Pratt

Lavender Cookbook: Essential Lavender Recipes

Lavender Cookbook: Simple & Delicious Recipes

A Colonial Tea – An historical one-act play

Daily Business Planner

Scone Recipes: Amazing Scone Baking Race

    Delicious, Prize-winning Scone Recipes

Tea Drinking in 18th Century America

Tea, its history and its mystery

Tea Journals – Series of five journal designs for Tea Shop Visits

Thank Goodness, It's Pie Day!

Education and Certification Classes:

Create+Design+Manage a Profitable Business ™

Tea Mastermind (membership/mentoring group)

Tea Mentor – STI Certification

"The best way to have a good idea is to have a lot of ideas." ~ Dr. Linus Pauling

ABOUT

Jennifer Petersen, Tea Trade Mart, is a business consultant and tea enthusiast with over 20 years as a tea blender, retail/wholesale business, and tea restaurant & gift shop owner. She is the owner and director of Tea Business School – Create+Design+Manage a Profitable Business™.

Ms. Petersen is a professional speaker and trainer recommended by the Specialty Tea Institute. She is a frequent speaker at international coffee and tea events and trade shows.

She is serves on the STI Advisory Board (Tea Council of the USA) and chaired the 2005 STI Tea Symposium in Seattle, Washington. She is co-chair of the STI Education Committee and serves on the marketing committee.

She is a member of the Specialty Tea Institute, Mid Atlantic Tea Business Association, Hawaii Tea Society, National Association of Christian Women Entrepreneurs, and Women Entrepreneurs Organization.

THANK YOU!

Thank you for purchasing the Weekly Journal, My Ideas Are As Bright as the Stars. I hope you enjoy implementing every page!

"The best way to have a good idea is to have a lot of ideas." ~ Dr. Linus Pauling

Made in the USA
Middletown, DE
14 April 2021